The Solar System

Exploring the Earth and Its Neighbors

This book helps children learn about some familiar elements of the universe. The celestial bodies that are the Earth's neighbors and that form the solar system are introduced here, through an imaginary adventure in which the children are the main characters. There is also a practical activity to be done with parents or teachers. This book is an interesting teaching tool for those just discovering the fascinating world of astronomy.

English translation of *The Solar System*
©Copyright 1998 by Barron's Educational Series, Inc.

©Copyright TREVOL PRODUCCIONS EDITORIALS S.C.P., 1998. Barcelona, Spain.

Original title of the book in Catalan: *El Sistema Solar, la Terra i els seus veïns.*

Address all inquiries to:
Barron's Educational Series, Inc.
250 Wireless Boulevard
Hauppauge, New York 11788
http://www.barronseduc.com

International Standard Book Number 0-7641-0685-6
Library of Congress Catalog Card Number 98-73390

Printed in Spain

98765432

The Solar System

Exploring the Earth and Its Neighbors

Text: Miquel Pérez   Illustrations: Maria Rius

BARRON'S

When we look up at the sky at night, we see a lot of tiny spots of light. Most of them are stars.

The sun is our star, one among the millions that form the universe. The sun is like a big shining lamp releasing light and warmth.

For years and years people have watched the sky at night. Through patient observation they discovered that some of the spots of light followed different paths from the stars. They called them planets.

We live on a planet—the Earth—and we have a small satellite traveling around us—the moon.

The Earth and the moon, together with the other planets and their moons, revolve around the sun. This group makes up the solar system.

"Attention! Do you want to explore the solar system? It's easy! Just use your imagination and pretend."

After a short time, our friends are flying in an orbit around the Earth.

"Wow, we are floating! The gravitational force no longer pulls us down toward the Earth."

"Look, half the Earth is lit up. It is daytime there. The other half is dark. It is nighttime there."

Thousands of miles from home, the spacecraft finally reaches the moon.

After a visit to our small satellite, the trip goes on.

"That's because we are getting closer to the sun, the largest celestial body in the solar system. The sun is a blazing star. We would melt if we got too close to it. That is what happens to comets. They are big pieces of ice and, when they get close to the sun, the top layer of ice starts to melt. Then they leave a long tail behind them."

Because of the heat, our friends have had to change their route and now they are heading toward the planets that are closest to the sun. They are small, rocky, and hot.

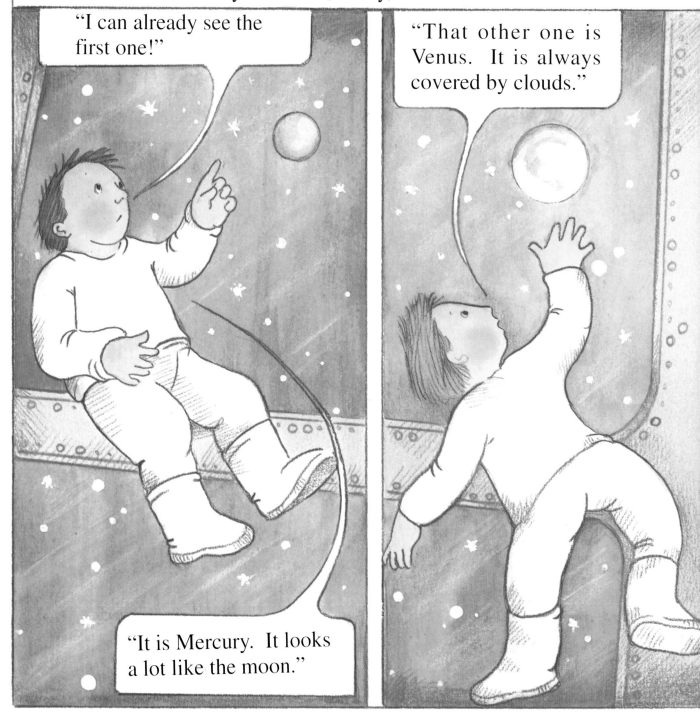

"I can already see the first one!"

"It is Mercury. It looks a lot like the moon."

"That other one is Venus. It is always covered by clouds."

Between Mars and the next planet, Jupiter, there are thousands of huge rocks floating in space. These rocks are called a belt of asteroids.

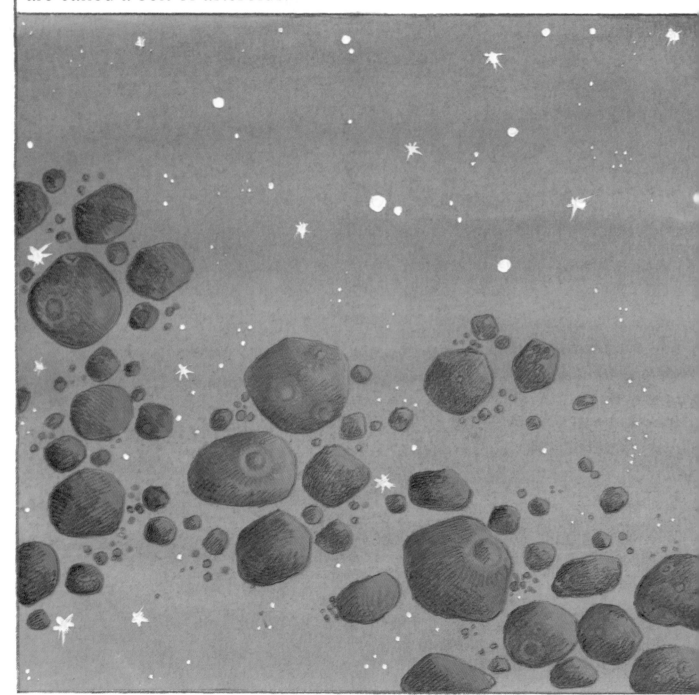

Beyond these floating rocks we can find the planets that are the farthest away from the sun. They are very far and very cold.

"What a huge planet and what a lot of moons it has!"

"That's Jupiter, called the giant plane_ And that other one has a ring around i_ as well as moons. It must be Saturn."

The trip was imaginary, but you can go to the planetarium and see and learn many wonderful things about the solar system.

A planetarium will show you all that we know about the entire universe!

Teaching activities and guidelines

This activity is designed to implement what has been learned from the book and to offer the children the chance to enjoy a nighttime outing with their parents or teachers.

First of all, we have to choose a clear night and drive far enough out of town so there will not be any lights to affect our vision. We will not see very much at first, but after about ten minutes, our eyes will grow used to the dark and we will start to see more and more stars.

Knowing some basics about astronomy can help us to better understand what we are seeing. We should know that the spots of light we see in the sky are mostly stars and some are planets. The planets, like the Earth, do not produce light of their own; we see them because their surfaces reflect the rays of the sun, as the moon does. Stars are self-luminous because they are huge balls of fire like our sun. Stars and planets are so far from the Earth, however, that we can only see them as tiny spots of light.

It is not easy to tell planets and stars apart. If we watched the sky for several days in a row, we would see that some of the spots of light change their position in relation to the others. Those are the planets, a name that in Greek means wanderer. But since the activity here is meant to take place in only one night, we will find another way to locate them.

Usually, any time of the year is good, although there are times when we can see virtually no planets. If we are lucky, however, we will be able to spot one not far from the horizon. We have to look for the brightest spots of light and, of these, the ones that do not twinkle. Jupiter, Mars, and Venus are the easiest ones to locate at first sight.

Jupiter is yellowish and, in theory, it should be the biggest and brightest spot of light we see. Like Saturn, Uranus, and Neptune, it is a gaseous giant with a lot of satellites and a belt around it, probably made of a great number of frozen rocks. Jupiter revolves about itself so fast that its day lasts only about ten hours. With the help of binoculars you can see four of its moons (see Figure 1), the same ones that Galileo discovered in 1609. Sometimes some of the moons are hidden by the planet itself.

1

Planet Mars, named for the Roman god of war, is a reddish color that resembles that of fire and blood. For a long time Mars was believed to be inhabited by strange beings, the Martians, but probes such as the Mariner, Viking, or the famous Pathfinder (see Figure 2), have made it clear that there is no life on the planet, even though they have discovered frozen water and carbon dioxide at its poles.

Venus is the first planet to be easily seen, although it disappears quickly. It comes out of the west just after sunset and from the east just before dawn. It honors the origin of its name, the Roman goddess of beauty, because it is a beautiful spectacle in itself. Sometimes it shines more than any other celestial body; sometimes, with the help of binoculars, we can see a crescent that resembles that of the moon. This happens because the orbits of both Venus and Mercury are closer to the sun than the orbit of the Earth.

2

The Earth is the only inner planet to have a satellite of its own—the moon. This is the first, and so far only, extraterrestrial object on which humans have set foot. Some theories claim that the moon was created by mingled terrestrial materials that had been thrown into space by the impact of a huge meteorite, but this is only a theory. It is very interesting to watch the moon through binoculars. When there is a full moon,

3

we can distinguish its craters from areas that are flat and dark (see Figure 3). When there is a crescent moon, we can see the relief of the craters in the area that separates day from night. When the new moon is only a few days away, the night area is not completely dark and it is possible to observe the whole lunar circle. This weak light is referred to as "ashen" light. It is the light of the sun reflected by the Earth.

Perhaps you have been fortunate enough to see a shooting star while being out at night, and you have probably thought that not everything up there is as stationary as it looks. Shooting stars are commonly considered to be stars that drop, but actually they are small pieces of interplanetary matter from some comet that fall into the Earth's atmosphere, where friction causes them to become incandescent and bright. If they are small enough, they melt and evaporate, but if they are large, they can fall to Earth and are then called meteorites. The most famous example is in Arizona, where there is a crater nearly a mile in diameter that was produced by the fall of a meteorite at least 20,000 years ago.

It is truly spectacular to make one of these nighttime excursions when the orbit of the Earth goes through an area where a lot of interplanetary matter is accumulated, around the 12th of August or the 14th of December. The media usually inform the public of the correct dates. During these nights of maximum activity, it is possible to see shooting stars quite frequently, a phenomenon known as a meteor shower (see Figure 4).

4